Devotions
and
Prayers of
F. B. Meyer

Compiled and edited
by Andrew Kosten

BAKER BOOK HOUSE
Grand Rapids, Michigan

INTRODUCTION

I first became acquainted with the writings of F. B. Meyer many years ago through the influence of devoutly religious parents. It is our belief that the evangelical writers our fathers found to be of great worth will also be cherished by their sons. This is one reason for adding the present volume to the Baker Devotional Series.

F. B. Meyer (1847-1929) was an outstanding religious writer, Bible expositor, and lecturer. Born in London and ordained in the Baptist church, Meyer authored a total of forty books, many of which have been reissued because of public demand. After fifteen years in the pastorate, he entered upon an extensive preaching mission to English-speaking countries, making a dozen such tours in the United States alone.

Many people believe that Dr. Meyer "never gave a mediocre exposition, never wrote a mediocre book." A more important and relevant judgment is to assert that Dr. Meyer has not been excelled in his devotional emphasis and in his beautiful prose style. His exposition of Isaiah—the source for the meditations of this volume—is one of his best books. The many readers of his expositions and longer books should welcome this classic. It is designed for ordinary people, for all members of a family.

This volume is—as every devotional work should be—small enough to be easily taken to the office or factory, or included in the luggage when travelling. In doing so you will find many opportunities to read it. The fifty-two devotions and matching prayers for the weeks of a year can help you make this a year-of-our-Lord in a vitally personal way.

Andrew Kosten

CONTENTS

Page

Introduction 3

1. Comfort Will Come 8
2. Home to the Heart 10
3. Human Weakness and Divine
Strength 12
4. Sacrifices and the Sacrifice 14
5. Unfailing Source of Renewal 16
6. The Sure Prophecy 18
7. The Poor in Spirit 20
8. The Motives of Men 22
9. Faithful in Little Things 24
10. Witness to a Love 26
11. You Will Have Trials 28
12. Design for Israel 30
13. Prayerlessness 32
14. Man—A Spiritual Being 34
15. Redemption and Sustenance
Through Death 36
16. Ever Dependent Upon God 38
17. Praying in Confidence 40
18. Every Knee Shall Bow 42
19. The Sustaining God 44
20. Antidote to Anxiety 46
21. The Divine Ideal 48
22. Summoned to an Exodus 50
23. Light to the Gentiles 52
24. The Shepherd's Care 54

25. A Mother's Love 56
26. Rest for the Weary 58
27. The Suffering Servant 60
28. Hope—Though but a Few 62
29. God Works for Eternity 64
30. Sleeper Awake! 66
31. Taking the Whole Armor 68
32. Beware Personal Babylons 70
33. Commandment of Purity 72
34. Jesus is the Key 74
35. The Mystery of Pain 76
36. The Arm of the Lord 78
37. Lifegiver for Moribund Man 80
38. Contrasts of the Cross 82
39. The Sinless Exception 84
40. Agony of Soul 86
41. The Satisfaction of Christ 88
42. The Majestic "I" 90
43. Consequences of Sin 92
44. Love Inalienable 94
45. Taught of God 96
46. God Rules and Overrules 98
47. Beyond Price 100
48. The Divine Call 102
49. The Road Back 104
50. Human and Divine Forgiveness 106
51. Restoration at Last 108
52. Transformed by Grace 110

Comfort Will Come

1

Comfort ye, comfort ye my people, saith your God — Isaiah 40:1.

COMFORT will come from God. It is well when meeting a friend to know by what route to expect him, lest he arrive on one platform while we await him on another. It is equally important to know in what quarter to look for comfort. Shall we look to the hills, the stable and lofty things of earth? No; in vain is salvation looked for from the multitude of the mountains. Shall we look to man? No, for he cannot reach low enough in the heart. Shall we look to the angels? No, God probably seldom sends them to comfort; perhaps they are too strong or they have never suffered. To bind up a broken heart requires a delicacy of touch which a Gabriel lacks. God reserves to himself the mission of comfort.

Comfort is a divine art. The choice name of the Son and the Spirit is Paraclete—the Consoler or Comforter. Yours is the God of all comfort.

Prayer

GREAT Saviour, who didst send the Comforter—for the temptations which he has overcome in us, for the comfort he has given us, for the fruits he has wrought in us, for the glimpses of thy love he has unfolded—I lovingly give thee thanks. Teach me the art of so living in fellowship with thee that every act may be a Psalm, every meal a sacrament, every room a sanctuary, and every thought a prayer. Amen.

Home to the Heart

2

Speak ye comfortably to Jerusalem, and cry unto her, that her welfare is accomplished, that her iniquity is pardoned; for she hath received of the Lord's hand double for all her sins — Isaiah 40:2.

T HE heart of regenerated man recognizes the voices that come from God; as a child, far from home in the blackest night, would recognize instantly any of the voices that it had been accustomed to hear from its cradle days.

This is one characteristic of the voices that reach us from God—"They speak home to the heart." This phrase in the Hebrew is the ordinary expression for wooing and describes the attitude of the suppliant lover attempting to win a maiden's heart. Love can detect love. The heart knows its true affinity. Many voices may speak to it, but it turns from them all until it hears the true note. In like manner you may recognize the voice of God. "I was asleep, but my heart waked; it is the voice of my Beloved that knocketh."

Prayer

HOLY Spirit, May my heart be filled with thy love, my lips with gentle, helpful words, and my hands with unselfish deeds. May those who see me take knowledge that I have been with Jesus. May the fragrance of his presence be shed abroad in every act. Amen.

Human Weakness and Divine Strength

3
All flesh is grass, and all the goodliness thereof is as the flower of the field — Isaiah 40:6b.

ALL flesh is grass and all its beauty like the wild flowers of the meadowlands, blasted by the breath of the the east wind or lying in swathes beneath the reaper's scythe. These words meet with a deep response in the heart of each thoughtful man. We have all seen it—our goodly sons, our sweet girls, our little babes have faded beneath our gaze. Jerusalem had long been in exile. One by one her heroes and defenders, her statesmen and prophets, had died in captivity. But listen further to the voices of the heavenly watchers.

The failure of man shall not frustrate the divine purpose. Lover and friend may stand aloof or be powerless to help. The strong arm may be unable to fulfill its former promises. The support of the family may be on his bed, incapable of maintaining his family. But God will do as he has said. He can make ravens bring food. "The grass withereth, the flower fadeth; but the word of the Lord shall stand for ever."

Prayer

THOU hast said, O Lord Jesus, that he that believeth in thee hath everlasting life. I do now believe. With my whole heart I look to thee as Saviour, friend, and king. In this glad hour I receive from thy hand not only life, but life more abundantly. Be thou my confidence and the center of my activities; and may I always be more conscious of thy presence than of the presence of others. Amen.

Sacrifices and the Sacrifice

4 And Lebanon is not sufficient to burn, nor the beasts thereof sufficient for a burnt-offering — Isaiah 40:16.

BEHIND us lie the hills, and beyond them the mountains, and above them all Lebanon rears her snow-capped peaks like a bank of clouds built up in the sky. But all the wood on Lebanon, its cedars riven with tempest and rugged with age, would not be too much to lay on the altar of Jehovah. And if all its beasts could be collected and laid on the wood in sacrifice, if Lebanon itself were the mighty altar of earth—there would be no extravagance in the vast burnt-offering that would fill the vault of heaven with fire and smoke.

So great is God that the greatest gifts of human self-denial, which have cost men most, are not too great. How preposterous, therefore, it is to liken him to any graven image or carving of wood! How needless to dread what men can do. How certain it is that he who spared not his own son, but gave him to a greater altar and fiercer flame, will with him also freely give us all things!

Prayer

OH, to have no thought closed from thy Spirit, no act other than thou wouldst approve, no word inconsistent with thy perfect love. Help me to remember, Heavenly Father, that what thou has given thou wilt also require. Enable me so to live that I may multiply the talents with which thou hast entrusted me, by using them for thy glory, and for the comfort and welfare of others. Amen.

Unfailing Source of Renewal

5

But they that wait upon the Lord shall renew their strength; they shall mount up with wings as eagles; they shall run, and not be weary; and they shall walk, and not faint — *Isaiah 40:31*.

MANY of us are too strong, self-reliant, and resourceful to get the best that God can give. But wait until your strength begins to faint beneath the burdens and the noon-tide heat; till the energy that was your boast had slowly ebbed away, and you are left without strength. Then the Mighty One of Jacob will draw near you and impart both power and strength.

They that wait on God renew their strength. It is new strength for each new duty or trial. As each fresh demand is made on them, they receive some unrealized enduement. Nothing, not even youthful genius and vigor, can be a substitute for this.

At first sight, it would appear that it should pass from walking to running, and from this to flying. But the order is reversed. To pursue the common track of daily duty—not faltering nor growing weary—to do so when novelty has worn off, when the elasticity of youth has vanished, when the applause of the crowd has become dim and faint—this is the greatest achievement of the Christian life.

Prayer

O MY Saviour, I am weary; the strain of life has exhausted me; the pressure of daily business has robbed me of my former energy. I have no strength even to cast my load. Forgive me for the lack of simple, childlike faith. Come near and rest me. Hush the fears I cannot allay; wipe the tears I cannot keep back. Lift me up, by thy strong arm, above the mists and darkness of the valley, to stand and walk with thee on the high level of thy manifested presence and glory. Amen.

The Sure Prophecy

6

Who raised up the righteous man from the east, called him to his foot, gave the nations before him, and made him rule over kings? He gave them as the dust to his sword, and as driven stubble to his bow — *Isaiah 41:2.*

Hᴵˢᵀᴼᴿʏ furnished some interesting confirmations of this contrast between the predictions of pagan oracles and the prophecies of the Old Testament Scripture. Herodotus, for example, tells us that when Croesus heard of the growing power of Cyrus, he was so alarmed for his kingdom that he sent rich presents to the oracles at Delphi and Dodona, asking what would be the outcome of his march. That at Delphi gave this ambiguous reply, that he would destroy a great empire. But whether the empire would be that of Cyrus or of Croesus was left unexplained. Whichever way the event turned, the oracle could claim to have predicted it.

How striking a contrast with the precise prediction of the Scripture, which gives us the name of the conqueror, the quarter from which he would fall upon Babylon, his reverence towards God, his simplicity and integrity of purpose!

Prayer

HASTEN the coming of thy kingdom, O Lord, the fulfillment of thy promise, and the consummation of thy purpose, that the travail of this world may soon usher in the rest of thy Sabbath. I know assuredly that all things are working together for my good; yet help me to wait patiently and toil diligently, though the waiting be long and the toil hard. Amen.

The Poor in Spirit

7

Fear thou not; for I am with thee: be not dismayed; for I am thy God: I will strengthen thee; yea, I will help thee; yea, I will uphold thee with the right hand of my righteousness — Isaiah 41:10.

NOT the wise and prudent, but the babes; not the high and mighty, but the lowly and obscure; not the king but the shepherd-lad: God finds them in their low estate, cast aside and disowned by the world, and adopting them, He makes for Himself a name and a praise.

It is necessary that God should have room in which to work. Emptiness to receive Him; weakness to be empowered by Him. It is into the empty branch that the vine sap pours; to the hollowed basin that the water flows. The weakness of the child gives scope for the man's strength. The need of the countless multitudes that thronged Christ's earthly life gave him opportunity for the working of his miracles, and the putting forth of his power. The prime blessedness of the kingdom of heaven is for the poor in spirit, the persecuted and the tempted, the wandering sheep, and the famishing child.

Prayer

HELP me to meditate more intently on thy humility and patience, O Lord, so that almost unconsciously these traits may appear in my own life. May I not be satisfied with talking or musing on thy love. Grant me the grace of manifesting it, not only in great crises, but amid petty annoyances and the daily fret. Amen.

8

GOD is always at work in our world, but his work is done so quietly, so unobstrusively, with such reticence as to his personal agency, that many affirm there is no God at all.

Are you concious that this is the temper of your soul, the quality of your work? If in your secret soul you seek the sweet voice of human adulation, if you are conscious of a wish to pass the results of your work into newspaper paragraph or to common talk of men, be sure that deterioration is fast corrupting your service, as rottenness the autumn fruit. It is high time then that you withdraw yourself to some lonely spot, where the silt that darkens the crystal waters of your soul may drop away, and again they mirror nothing but the sky with its depths of blue, its hosts of stars.

The only work that God approves, that is permanent and fruitful, that partakes of the nature of Christ is that which neither seeks nor needs advertisement.

Prayer

Lord Jesus, we thank thee that a new day affords another opportunity for consecration and devotion. Thou hast turned a fresh page in our life's story. It comes from thee without blemish or soil; help us to keep it so. Forgive the past blotted with our failures and sins, and help us to walk in the light. I cannot hope to sit on thy right or thy left in thy kingdom, but at least permit me to sit at thy feet and hear thy word. Amen.

Faithful in Little Things

9

A bruised reed shall he not break, and the smoking flax shall he not quench: he shall bring forth judgment unto truth—Isaiah 42:3.

FANNING the spark of the smoking flax until that which had nearly died out in the heart of a Peter sets on fire three thousand souls within seven weeks of its threatened extinction. This is the test of true work. Where does it find you? Are you ambitious for a larger sphere, grudging the pains needed to explain the gospel to the ignorant, to cope with the constant relapses of the weak, to combat the fears of the timorous and mistrustful, to adjust the perpetual disputes and quarrels of newly-made disciples, to suit your pace to the weakest and youngest of the flock? Beware; your work is in danger of losing its noblest quality; the hue is passing from the summer fruit; the tender tone which God loves is fading from your picture; the grace of the day is dying. Before it is too late, consider that the noblest souls are sometimes found within bruised bodies, and the greatest work often emanates from the most inconspicious sparks.

Prayer

HOLY Spirit, may my heart be filled with thy love. Make me humble and unselfish. Give me a childlike faith to receive what thou dost offer and to bear what thou dost ordain. Make me fruitful in every good work to do thy will. Thou hast given me yearnings after a holy life; accomplish them by thy grace dwelling within me and working through me continually. Amen.

10

But now thus saith the Lord that created thee, O Jacob, and he that formed thee, O Israel, Fear not: for I have redeemed thee, I have called thee by thy name; thou art mine — *Isaiah 43:1.*

FEAR not! thou art mine!" The words are very simple. They would come to a little lost child from a mother's lips as she again embraced it. It is much for you, O exiled soul, robbed and spoiled, that God still calls you his. He will not stay his hand until he elicits the response, "Great and Good God, thou art mine!" Neither sin nor sorrow can cut with their accursed shears the knot of union which the divine fingers have tied between your weak soul and the everlasting Lover of men.

"Precious." Israel hardly dared to think it. And certainly no observer unacquainted with the ways of God could dare suppose that Jehovah counted his people as his priceless treasure. But, nevertheless, the words stand out clearly. Yes, soul of man, you are the pearl of great price, to obtain which the merchantman in search of priceless jewels sold all that he had and bought the world in which you did lie like a common pebble.

Prayer

CAUSE me, O God, to be inflamed with
heavenly desires, and may thy love be so
shed abroad in my heart that I may evermore seek the things which are above.
There is nothing in me that can attract or
hold thy love. I have failed so often and
cost thee so much. Forgive the bitter past.
May I receive the abundance of thy grace
and reign in life here and hereafter. Amen.

You Will Have Trials

When thou passest through the waters, I will be with thee; and through the rivers, they shall not overflow thee: When thou walkest through the fire, thou shalt not be burned; neither shall the flame kindle upon thee — Isaiah 43:2.

11

GOD does not keep his children from the waters and the fire. We might have expected the verse to run, "Thou shalt never pass through the waters, or through the river; thou shalt never have to walk through the fire." But so far from this, it seems taken as a matter of course that there will be the waters and the fire; the overflowing floods of sorrow; the biting flame of sarcasm and hate. God's people are not saved from trial, but in it. Fire and water are cleansing agents that cannot be dispensed with. The gold and silver, the brass, iron, and tin — everything that can abide the fire—must go through the fire, that it may be clean; and that which cannot abide the fire must go through the water.

Sometimes the world wonders at seeing God's people in trouble as other men—not knowing that the King Himself has passed through flood and flame; not knowing also that there are fords for the floods and paths through the fire.

Prayer

KEEP me through this day from all that would grieve thy Holy Spirit. Help me to look not on the dark cloud but on the rainbow, not on the stormy waters but on the face of Jesus, not on my own fickle heart but on thy love. Keep me from running hither and yon for human sympathy. May I be satisfied with thine. Whom have I in heaven but thee, and on earth none is to be desired beside thee. Amen.

Design for Israel

This people have I formed for myself, they shall show forth my praise — Isaiah 43:21.

JEHOVAH'S design is clearly declared in the significant passage that heads this chapter—"They shall show forth my praise." By a long process of careful training, it was his intention so to form the people that their history should turn men's thoughts to the glory and beauty of his own nature, and elicit perpetual adoration and praise. They were to go forth throughout the world teaching men the love and goodness of him who had found them in the waste howling wilderness and had made them a nation of priests and of sweet psalmists.

By repeated failure the Jews set themselves against the accomplishment of the divine plan. And on three separate occasions they had to learn the temporary suspension and postponement of his purpose. In the meanwhile the Gentiles have been called to take their place with blessed results, until the branches which were broken off are again grafted into their olive-tree.

Prayer

LORD Jesus, as thou didst love Jerusalem, teach me to love my fatherland. I pray for our ruler and the rulers of other lands—for statesmen, judges, and all in authority—that we may be godly governed. May peace and happiness, justice and truth, be established among us for all generations. Amen.

Prayerlessness

But thou hast not called upon me, O Jacob; but thou hast been weary of me, O Israel — *Isaiah 43:22.*

NOTHING is as sure a gauge of our spiritual state as our prayers. There may be a weariness of the brain which is the reaction of overstrain, and against which it is not wise to struggle. When mind and heart are so overpowered by the fatigues of the body that an inevitable drowsiness closes the eye and restrains the flow of thought, it is better to say, as we yield ourselves to sleep, "O Lord, we are on the same terms as yesterday." But this is very different from the perfunctory and hurried devotions which arise from the preoccupation of the mind in things of time and sense, or the alienation of the heart from God by sin. If this lethargy is stealing over you, beware!

Probably none of us goes wrong at first in the breach of the great obligations of the law. It is the little rift in the lute, the tiny speck in the fruit, the small orifice in the bank where deterioration begins. But nothing is small that concerns God or the soul.

Prayer

ALMIGHTY God, teach me the dignity of labor, the honor of industrious toil, the glory of being able to do something in the world. Forgive, I pray thee, my shortcomings and failure, prosper and establish the work of my hands. Make my life deeper, stronger, richer, gentler, more Christlike, more full of the spirit of Heaven, more devoted to thy service and glory. Amen.

Man — A Spiritual Being

14

Remember these, O Jacob and Israel; for thou art my servant: I have formed thee; thou art my servant: O Israel, thou shalt not be forgotten of me — *Isaiah 44:21*.

THE true dignity of man betrays itself in the hunger which perpetually preys upon him. If man is only matter, if thought is only the movement of the grey matter of the brain, if there is no spirit and no beyond, how is it that the material world cannot supply the supreme good? and that when, as in the case of Solomon, life is filled with all that wealth and power can yield, man turns from it all as a vain and empty bubble, the mirage of the desert, the apples of Sodom, the chaff which cannot appease hunger? Does not this show that there are component parts of man's nature, and these the noblest, which, because they cannot be appeased by the contents of the time-sphere, are above time, and belong to the eternal and unseen? Must not there be something divine in man, if he hungers for the divine—something spiritual and eternal, since the spiritual and eternal alone can meet his need?

Prayer

MY Father, help me to find my life according to thy promise. Leave me not nor forsake me in the toilsome, upward climb. Teach me to change my strength and mount up with the wings of eagles. May the Holy Spirit enable me to realize in daily life my true position in Christ. Where he is, may I in heart and mind continually ascend and habitually dwell. Amen.

15

I have blotted out, as a thick cloud, thy transgressions, and, as a cloud, thy sins: return unto me; for I have redeemed thee — Isaiah 44:22.

NATURE yields her provision to man through death. The standing corn is mowed down by the sickle; the cattle fall beneath the staggering blow or the gash of the knife. For the wild things of the forest there are the rifle and swift death. So it is through death that Jesus has become the food of men.

The Lord's Supper perpetually reminds us of this. The bread and wine that nourish us there are the emblems of the flesh and the blood of one who has died and is risen again. At that holy feast we commemorate the death of one who lives forever; and show forth that the life which nourishes our spirits had passed through the sharpness of death, that it might nourish within our spirits the eternal life. Our Lord's repeated reference to flesh and blood enforces and accentuates this truth—that it is only through his death, and through our participation with him of death, that he can become the true meat and the true drink.

Prayer

FATHER of Jesus, give me that same Holy Spirit that raised him from the dead that he may raise me from the dead. I long that his risen life may be more evidently mine; and that I may experience the power of his resurrection, rising as a fountain in my soul. Send thy Holy Spirit into the world to convict men of sin and righteousness and judgment. May he work again as at Pentecost, that thousands may be stricken to the heart and many times of refreshing come from thy presence. Amen.

Ever Dependent Upon God

16

That they may know from the rising of the sun, and from the west, that there is none beside me. I am the Lord, and there is none else — *Isaiah 45:6*.

GOD ever girds for tasks to which he calls. He cannot desert what had cost him so much. He will finish what he had begun. He will lead you over crag and torrent until the night is gone.

When Peter stood with Jesus by the shores of the lake of Galilee he contrasted the independence of his earliest days, when he walked whither he would, with the dependence of those later days when he should stretch forth his hands and another should support him. With these words our Lord signified the manner of death in which he should glorify God. What was true of the helplessness of Peter's old age and martyrdom should be true of each of us in the intention and choice of the soul. Let us give up girding ourselves in the assertion of our own strength, and stretch forth our hands, asking our Lord to gird us and carry us whither he will, even to death, if thereby we may the better glorify God.

Prayer

ALMIGHTY God, thou knowest my great
need. Graciously draw near to me and cover
my head in the day of battle, that those
evils which the craft and subtlety of the
devil or man worketh against me may be
brought to naught, and by thy goodness be
dispersed. Keep me outwardly in my body
and inwardly in my soul, that I may be de-
fended from all adversities which may hap-
pen to the body, and from all evil thoughts
which may assault the soul. Amen.

Praying in Confidence

17

Thus saith the Lord, the Holy One of Israel, and his Maker, Ask me of things to come concerning my sons, and concerning the work of my hands command ye me — *Isaiah 45:11*.

IT is a marvellous relationship into which God bids us enter. We are accustomed to obey him. We are familiar with words like those that follow: "I, even My hands have stretched out the heavens, and all their host have I commanded." But that God should invite us to command him! This is a change in relationship which is startling. But there is no doubt as to the literal force of these words. With the single limitation that our biddings must concern his sons, and the work of his hands, and must be included in his word of promise, Jehovah says to us, his redeemed children in Jesus Christ, "Command ye me."

What a difference there is between this attitude and the hesitating, halting, unbelieving prayers to which we are accustomed, and which by their repetition lose edge and point! Long familiarity with him even affected the speech of the apostles; for in their Spirit-inspired prayers we can detect this same tone of confidence.

Prayer

I THANK thee, O God, that thy blessed Son was manifested that he might destroy the works of the devil and bring us into fellowship with himself. Deliver me, I pray thee, from evil and purify me even as Christ is pure. I claim from thee the fulfillment of thy covenant promise, that thou shouldst write thy law upon my heart and remember my sins and iniquities no more. May I hear thee say, "Go, and sin no more; thy faith hath saved thee." Amen.

Every Knee Shall Bow

18

I have sworn by myself, the word is gone out of my mouth in righteousness, and shall not return, That unto me every knee shall bow, every tongue shall swear — *Isaiah 45:23.*

YIELD yourself to God, O soul of man! Whatever he says to you, do it. Be careful even to details in your obedience. Let God have his way with you. In proportion as you will yield to him, you shall have power with God. The more absolutely you are a man under authority to the Commander-in-Chief, the more you shall be able to say to this and the other of his resources.

But after our greatest deeds of prayer and faith, we should lie low before God, as Elijah did. After calling fire from Heaven, Elijah prostrated himself on the ground with his face between his knees. The mightiest angels of God's presence bend the lowest; the holiest souls present perpetually the sacrifice of the broken and contrite spirit. The power to move the arm that moves the world is wielded by those who can most humbly adopt the confession — "I am a worm, and no man."

Prayer

HEAVENLY Father, send forth the tidings of thy salvation to the ends of the earth. Be with thy missionaries, who are engaged in preaching the gospel to mankind. Turn the hearts of all men towards Christ and make them obedient to the faith. Hasten the time when all creation shall be delivered from the bondage of corruption to the glorious liberty of thy children. May thy purpose be speedily accomplished in thy Church. Amen.

The Sustaining God

19

And even to your old age I am he; and even to hoar hairs will I carry you: I have made, and I will bear; even I will carry, and will deliver you — Isaiah 46:4.

JEHOVAH speaks to the house of Jacob, and to all the remnant of the house of Israel, as children whom he has borne from the birth and carried from earliest childhood. Their God needed not to be borne, he bore; needed no carriage, since his everlasting arms made cradle and carriage both. Such as he had been, he would be. He would not change. He would carry them, even to hoary hairs. He had made and he would bear; he would carry and deliver. This contrast is a perpetual one.

Some people carry their religion; other people are carried by it. Some are burdened by the prescribed creeds, ritual, observances, exactions, to which they believe themselves to be committed. Others have neither thought of nor cared for those things. They have yielded themselves to God and are persuaded that he will bear them and carry them as a man does his son in all the way that they go.

Prayer

COMFORTER of the comfortless, bind my soul with thine in intercession. Wherever there are broken hearts, bind them; captives, release them; smoking flax, fan its spark; bruised reeds, make them pillars in thy temple. Bless especially my loved ones and those who misunderstand me. Visit them with thy salvation and suit thy gifts to their particular needs. Amen.

20

THE sin is our own. In no sense can the sinner lay it on God. "I have sinned," man cries, "and perverted that which was right, and it did not profit me. The sin is mine." And yet from the depth of sin-consciousness there is an appeal to God. He created, permitted us to be born as members of a sinful race. He knew all we should be, before he set his heart upon us and made us his own. May we not ask him to bear with us whom he made, redeemed, and took to be his children by adoption and grace?

When burdened with care for ourselves and others, we fall at the foot of the altar-steps that slope through darkness to God. When our circumstances are beyond measure perplexing, when we have no idea what to do, or how to act for the best—is there not every reason to look into the face of God and say, "Thou hast permitted me to come hither, thou alone knowest what I should do."

Prayer

HEAVENLY Father, deliver me I pray
thee from the fear of man that bringeth a
snare. May I fear thee alone with the reverence born of love. Thou art stirring up my
nest and the old is changing and giving
place to the new. Spread therefore thy wings
beneath me, I pray, and teach me to trust
where I can see no earthly support to rest
upon. Amen.

The Divine Ideal

21

O that thou hadst hearkened to my commandments! then had thy peace been as a river, and thy righteousness as the waves of the sea — *Isaiah 48:18.*

WALK along the beach when the tide had ebbed, mark the wastes of sand, the muddy ooze, the black unsightly rocks. Not thus did God intend that any of his children should be. It was never his will that their righteousness should ebb, that there should be wastes, and gaps, and breaks in their experience, that there should be the fatal lack of strength, and purity, and virtue. The divine ideal of the inner life is mid-ocean, where the waves reach to the horizon on every side, and there are miles of sea-water beneath. No one can look on the majestic roll of the Atlantic breakers without realizing the magnificence of the divine intention that all who have learned to call God Father should be possessed of a moral nature, which is as pure in its character as those waves which far out to sea proclaim the power of God.

Prayer

LORD God Almighty, how shall I ever sufficiently thank thee for adopting me into thy family and making me one of thy children! Thou hast taught me to know thee, pray to thee, and love thee. Thou art my shield and my exceeding great reward. Let the great cloud of witnesses, who have gone before and entered into their rest, be to me for an example of a godly life, and even now may I be refreshed with their joy and run with patience the remainder of the race that is set before me. Amen.

Summoned to an Exodus

22

Go ye forth of Babylon, flee ye from the Chaldeans, with a voice of singing declare ye, tell this, utter it even to the end of the earth; say ye, The Lord hath redeemed his servant Jacob — *Isaiah 48:20*.

THIS summons for an Exodus rings out to the Church of the living God from the heavenly watchers—"Come forth out of her, my people, that ye be not partakers of her sins, and that ye receive not of her plagues." And in the words that follow there is an evident reference to the overthrow of Babylon, with an application to the godless system of human society which confronts the Church in every age.

By his intellect and energy man is still endeavoring to rear a structure independently of God, to make himself a name and defy the waters of time's deluge from sweeping away his work. All human imaginings, strivings, energizings, man's ceaseless activities, the outcome of human life, apart from the spirit of God, constitute a fabric as real as that of Babel or Babylon the Great, though no material fabric arises as its visible memorial.

Prayer

I PRAY, O Heavenly Father, for those who are wandering from thy ways in darkness and error. Have mercy upon them and convert them to thyself. Rekindle in them the flame of thy pure love and restore them to their former joy, that they may praise thee for thy recovering mercy. Thou art the door, O Lord. Through thee may I pass out to my daily work and back again to rest. And whether in work or in rest, may I abide in thy keeping. Amen.

Light to the Gentiles

23

And he said, it is a light thing that thou
shouldest be my servant to raise up the
tribes of Jacob, and to restore the pre-
served of Israel: I will also give thee for a
light to the Gentiles, that thou mayest be
my salvation unto the end of the earth —
Isaiah 49:6.

THESE words were expressly referred to
Jesus Christ by his great apostle on one of
the most memorable occasions in his career.
The little synagogue at Antioch was crowd-
ed to its doors, for the city was eager to
hear the stranger. But the Jews were filled
with jealousy and "contradicted the things
which were spoken by Paul and Barnabas,
and blasphemed." After a while the preach-
er realized that the terms of his commission
did not require him to expend his words on
those who refused them; so he suddenly
changed his note.

He had made an offer of eternal life,
which had been rejected with disdain; there
was nothing left but to turn to the Gentiles, and he quoted the climax words of
this paragraph in defense of the course he
hereupon adopted. "For so hath the Lord
commanded us, saying, I have set thee for
a light to the Gentiles, that thou shouldest
be for salvation unto the uttermost part of
the earth."

Prayer

O THOU who hast the key of David, who openeth and no man shutteth, who shuttest and no man openeth; go before me today, I pray thee, opening shut gates that I may pass through them to fulfill thy purpose in my life. Help me to take up my cross and follow thee in thy humiliation and faith, so that I may at length behold thy face in righteousness and receive from thee that crown which fadeth not away. Amen.

The Shepherd's Care

24

They shall not hunger nor thirst; neither shall the heat nor the sun smite them: for he that hath mercy on them shall lead them, even by the springs of water shall he guide them — Isaiah 49:10.

Y OU can detect the accent of the true shepherd in Jacob's excuse for not accompanying the rapid march of Esau and his warriors. "The flocks and herds with me give suck, and if they overdrive them one day, all the flocks will die. I will lead on softly, according to the pace of the cattle that is before me."

All this and much more is summed up in the exceedingly beautiful words, "He that hath mercy on them shall lead them." What comfort is here! He knows our frame. He is touched with the feeling of our infirmities; he will not over-drive us. He will go before and lead us, but he will suit his pace to ours. The severest strain shall not overtax our powers. However rough and difficult the path, ever remember that thou art being led by him who had mercy on you. Hunger and thirst will be impossible for those who abide in his care and fellowship. Are you enveloped in shadow? It is only lest heat and sun smite you.

Prayer

O MY Father, I know that thou lovest me, and that thy love has chosen my path. I would have it so. Help me to be satisfied with thy wise choice of time and tide, of sun and shower. Grant unto me such faith in thy fatherly mercy and love that I may never be troubled about the things of this life, but seek the coming of thy kingdom and the glory of our Lord. Amen.

A Mother's Love

25

Can a woman forget her sucking child, that she should not have compassion on the son of her womb? yea, they may forget, yet will I not forget thee — *Isaiah 49:15.*

MANY devout but misguided persons have placed the Virgin Mother almost on a level with God, and worship her, because they think that woman is more tender, more patient, more forgiving than man.

Of human love, none is so pure, so unselfish, so full of patient brooding pity, as a mother's. And that love follows us through life—often repelled and unrequited. It lingers near us in prayers and tears and holy yearnings. At the first symptom of illness or distress it hurries to our side. It will stand by the felon in the dock and hunt for a girl through Sodom.

Such love is God's. Indeed it is a ray from his heart. If a mother's love is but the ray, what must his heart be. But there is sometimes a failure in motherhood. "They may forget." Maddened with frenzy, flushed with unholy passion, infatuated with the giddy round of gaiety, a woman has been known to forget her child. The fires on all human altars may have burnt to white ash; but God's love will be what it was when first we knew him.

Prayer

MERCIFUL Saviour, help me to pray for thy one family scattered in all lands, especially for those who are united to me by the tenderest bonds of nature or love. Encompass them with thy tender care. Keep them from harm and sin, and from too great sorrow amid the discipline of their lives. Take me as I return home to thee, soiled and dusty with the sin and business of the day. Cleanse me from all unrighteousness, not only with the grace of forgiveness, but with the grace that passes through every chamber of the inner life, purifying and sanctifying. Amen.

Rest for the Weary

26

The Lord God hath given me the tongue of the learned, that I should know how to speak a word in season to him that is weary: he wakeneth morning by morning, he wakeneth my ear to hear as the learned — Isaiah 50:4.

ALL souls at some part of their life get weary. There is nothing new about this, but the novelty consists in the infinite care that God takes of the weary. There is nothing like it outside the Bible, and the literature to which it has given birth. Man hears with composure that scores of weary ones have fallen out of the march of human life, and lie stretched on the scorching sand, doomed to expire of fatigue and thirst. God, on the other hand, stoops to the need of the weakling, expends his care on the lame, halt, maimed, and blind; adopts into his family those who had been rejected for their deformities and ugliness; gathers up the broken fragments; tills the sterile ground, ransacks the highways and byways for the strays whom no one invites to his board. And he is perpetually engaged in brooding over each weary heart with its sore, its tears, its yearnings, its despair. This God is our God forever, unrivalled in his tender pity, the God of the fatherless and the widow.

Prayer

OF thine infinite mercy, O Lord, deliver me from the terror by night and the arrow that flieth by day, from the pestilence that walketh in darkness and from the destruction that wasteth at noonday; that leaning on thine aid, comforted by thy grace, I may dwell in peace and safety. Amen.

The Suffering Servant

27

I gave my back to the smiters, and my cheeks to them that plucked off the hair: I hid not my face from shame and spittng —
Isaiah 50:6.

ON one occasion towards the close of his earthly ministry, when the fingers of the dial-plates were pointing to the fulfillment of time, we are told that he set his face stedfastly to go to Jerusalem. What heroism was here! Men sometimes speak of Christ as if he were effeminate and weak, deficient in manly courage, and remarkable only for passive virtues. But such conceptions are refuted by the indomitable resolution which sets its face like a flint, and knew that it would not be ashamed.

Note the voluntariness of Christ's surrender. The martyr dies because he cannot help it. Christ died because he chose to. He laid down his life of himself; no one took it from him. He might have been rebellious and turned away backward, or called for twelve legions of angels, or pinned his captors to the ground by recourse to his inherent God-head. But he did not. It is this that stirs our hearts with admiration and devotion, as we see him deliberately giving his back to the smiters.

Prayer

MY Master and my Lord, may I know that thou goest before as of old, before thy disciples. The sword pierces thy heart before it touches mine, and the waves spend themselves on thee before I am wetted by their spray. The heavy part of my cross rests on thee. Amen.

Hope — Though But a Few

28

Look unto Abraham your father, and unto Sarah that bare you: for I called him alone, and blessed him, and increased him—*Isaiah 51:2.*

THE nation was greatly reduced in numbers and the godly were but a handful. It seemed preposterous to suppose that they would ever attain to such prolific numbers as to rival the sands on the shore or the stars of space. The tree had been so mercilessly cut down, and pruned, that they despaired of again beholding its spreading branches, laden with fruit. In answer to such forebodings the voice of inspiration cries, "Look back! Consider Abraham and Sarah. There was a time when they were the sole representatives of the Hebrew race; yet of them and of the one son of their old age came countless people. What little cause, then, is there for fear? Though you were reduced to a single aged pair, these might become the origin of a mighty nation. How much more is there reason for hope now that you may still be counted by your thousands."

Prayer

ALMIGHTY God, thy faithfulness reacheth unto the skies—help me to reckon upon it in every step of this day's pilgrimage. Thy righteousness is like the great mountains. May I keep in view of it always. Make me to hate evil and to cleave to that which is good. Take from me the heart of stone and deliver me from idols. Take from me the love of sin. Put thy Spirit within me and cause me to walk in thy way. Amen.

God Works For Eternity

29

For the moth shall eat them up like a garment, and the worm shall eat them like wool: but my righteousness shall be for ever, and my salvation from generation to generation — Isaiah 51:8.

WHEN we partake of God's righteousness, and assimilate it, we acquire a permanence which defies time and change. The love we derive from the heart of God and have for each other abides forever. The peace we receive deepens in its perennial flow. The patience, courage, strength of character, which we acquire here with so much pain, are not to go out as a candle, nor vanish as a puff of smoke. If it were so, what would become of God's concern?

No, our school may be in ruins and not a vestige of it remain, but the characters we acquired shall outlive the world of matter. These shall be forever and shall not be abolished. Oh, let us not murmur at the slow progress of our education and at the care that God takes for us to master each lesson—turning it back, making us review it again and again. He is working for eternity.

Prayer

GRACIOUS God, forgive the past; keep me as the apple of thine eye. Encompass me with thy care and realize in me thy highest purposes. So will I offer in thy tabernacles sacrifices of joy. May thy word be increasingly precious to me. In thy words may I ever hear the word. Beholding thy face in this mirror may I be changed. Amen.

Sleeper Awake!

30

Awake, awake, put on thy strength, O Zion; put on thy beautiful garments, O Jerusalem, the holy city: for henceforth there shall no more come into thee the uncircumcised and the unclean — *Isaiah 52:1*.

THE somnolent city of Zion thought God had been asleep, and called on him to awake. She had to learn that it was not so. It was she that had been sleeping; and therefore the appeal was flashed back from God to her, "Awake, awake, put on thy strength, O Zion; put on thy beautiful garments, O Jerusalem."

There are other soporifics than the wrath of God: the air of the enchanted ground; the laudanum of evil companionship; the drugs of worldly pleasure, of absorption in business, of cruel security. By these we are all liable to be thrown into a deep sleep. The army of the Lord is too apt to put off the armor of light and resign itself to heavy slumbers till the clarion voice warns that it is time to awake. We too lose the ardour of our zeal, the warmth of our love and become benumbed and insensible. Then we start from our slumber thinking that God had been asleep, whereas it was ourselves.

Prayer

MAKE me very sensitive to perceive thee, my Lord and Master, to hear thy voice and to receive those gracious gifts from thee. May the Holy Spirit glorify thee, taking of things that are thine and revealing them unto me. Thou, O Lord, dost not despair of the most ignorant and unworthy. Heal and save and teach me, I pray. Amen.

Taking the Whole Armor

31

Shake thyself from the dust; arise, and sit down, O Jerusalem: loose thyself from the bands of thy neck, O captive daughter of Zion — *Isaiah 52:2.*

GOD provides strength for every emergency or demand in life. Whatever call is made upon us, there is always a sufficiency of grace by which it may be met. Undoubtedly, temptation and trial are permitted to come so that we may be compelled to appropriate supplies which lie within our reach, but of which we should not have availed ourselves, unless hard pressed and put to it.

We are not asked to purchase strength or generate it by our resolutions, prayers, and agonizings; but to put it on. Before passing from the quiet morning hour into the arena which has so often witnessed failure and defeat, put on the might of the risen Saviour. Do not simply pray to be kept or to be helped; but arm yourself with the whole armor of God. Take hold of his strength and be at peace. Wrap yourself about with the mail of him who is stronger than the strong man armed.

Prayer

HOLY Father, give me grace to lay aside the works of darkness and to put on the armor of light. May all self-indulgence, all that is earthly, selfish, and unholy be put away, and may I not fail thee in the day of battle. If it is thy will that temptation should come upon me today, may I not distrust thy leading hand, nor think that failure is inevitable, nor concern myself overmuch with our great adversary. Be with me when I am surrounded by the wild beasts and let angels minister. Amen.

32

Thy watchmen shall lift up the voice; with the voice together shall they sing: for they shall see eye to eye, when the Lord shall bring again Zion — *Isaiah 52:8.*

IN all lives there are Babylons, which have no claim on the redeemed of Jehovah. We may have entered them, not without qualms of conscience; but as time has passed, our reluctance has been overcome. A comradeship has grown up between us and one from whose language and ways we once shrank in horror. An amusement now fascinates us, which once we regarded with conscientious scruple. A habit of life dominates us from which we once shrank as from infection. These are Babylons which cast their fatal spell over the soul and against which the voice of God urgently protests.

When stepping out from Babylon to an unwonted freedom, we naturally shrink back before the desert march, the sandy wastes, the ruined remnants of happier days. But we shall receive more than we renounce. Forsaking the outward and temporal, we shall find ourselves possessed of the inner and eternal.

Prayer

HEAVENLY Father, fence me round
with thy protecting care. Thou knowest
how I wait for footsteps that do not come;
yearn for a sympathy which is withheld;
knock at doors that do not open; and dread
what tomorrow may bring. I shrink from
the loneliness of life and the mystery of
that unknown future that stretches away
in the dark like a moor beyond the light of
home. But nothing can separate me from
thee. Amen.

Commandment of Purity

33

Depart ye, depart ye, go ye out from thence, touch no unclean thing; go ye out of the midst of her; be ye clean, that bear the vessels of the Lord — *Isaiah 52:11*.

THOSE vessels we know were very precious as the enumeration is made with minute accuracy (Ezra 8:26). But they were above all things holy unto the Lord. For generations they had been employed in temple service. Those that bore them were no common men, but Levites specially summoned to the work and possessed at least of a ceremonial cleanliness. Thus they passed across the desert, holy men bearing the holy vessels.

Through this world, unseen by mortal eye, a procession is passing, threading its way across continents of time. It bears holy vessels. The forms of expression in which divine truth is enshrined may be compared to the vessels of the old dispensation, set apart to serve the purposes of the sanctuary. Testimony to God's truth, the affirmation of things unseen and eternal, the announcement of the facts of redemption— such are our sacred charge. We must contend earnestly for the faith once delivered to the saints. Take heed to yourself.

Prayer

Have mercy upon me, most merciful Father, and for the sake of Jesus Christ forgive my sins and take away all iniquity. May I henceforth serve thee in newness of life. I humbly ask that the Holy Spirit may open my eyes more fully to behold and my heart more ardently to love thee in him, who is the brightness of thy glory, the express image of thy person. Amen.

Jesus Is the Key

34 Behold, my servant shall deal prudently, he shall be exalted and extolled, and be very high — *Isaiah 52:13.*

JESUS is the key which the New Testament in many allusions puts into our hands to unlock these mysteries, in which heaven and earth, the eternal and the temporal, the love of God and the weakness of man blend, with no apparent horizon line. But even apart from this precise testimony of the Holy Spirt, we could have found none worthy to take the scroll and open it seal by seal, but the lamb in the midst of the throne, the Son of God.

Efforts have been made to apply this or the other line and fragment of this prophecy to one and another of the great sufferers of history—to Jeremiah, to Ezekiel, to some unknown martyr in the days of the captivity. And no wonder, for sorrow and pain are the heritage of all. In some particulars this vision may have been realized by lesser men than the Son of Man. But who of woman born, but the Christ, could take these words in their entirety and say—"I claim that all this was realized in myself; this portrait is mine."

Prayer

LORD JESUS, I pray for thy Church, the members of which are scattered in many different sects and over the wide world. They who are one with thee must be one with each other. Hasten in all lands thy reign. May all kings bow down before thee, all nations serve thee. Amen.

The Mystery of Pain

35

As many were astonished at thee; his visage was so marred more than any man, and his form more than the sons of men — Isaiah 52:14.

A SUGGESTION of the anguish which our Lord endured is given in those remarkable words of the epistle to the Hebrews, which tell us that after pouring out his prayers and supplications with strong crying and tears unto him who was able to save him from death, he was heard in that he feared.

In every age Christian men have pondered those words, asking what they meant. Is it not possible for Jesus to have meant that he was so wrung with anguish that he thought he must die in the garden before he reached his cross? The pressure of pain was almost unendurable and there was the fear that his nature would collapse before the sacrifice could be offered. If this is the right rendering of the passage, what a marvelous conception is afforded of the suffering which surged up and rolled over the human nature of the Redeemer! If the anticipation of Calvary so wrung his heart, what must the actual experience have been? Such was the mystery of pain.

Prayer

MOST gracious God, wherever at this hour there is sore sickness in home or hospital; wherever souls are passing from time into eternity; wherever there is anguish, peril, and alarm, there may thy Holy Spirit instill peace and help. I ask it in the name of Jesus Christ. Amen.

The Arm of the Lord

36 Who hath believed our report? and to whom is the arm of the Lord revealed? — *Isaiah 53:1.*

THE life of the Son of Man appeared from many points of view to be a failure. The arm of the Lord was in him, though hidden from all save the handful who believed. Probably our Lord never wrought a miracle unless faith was exercised on the part either of the recipients or spectators of his saving help. The centurion, though a Gentile, the Syrophoenician woman, though accounted a dog, the leper though an outcast pariah—drew from him virtue that healed and saved. While the bulk of the nation, especially the companions of his early life, missed the benediction, which had come so nigh them, because they stood aloof in proud indifference. Through unbelief the branches were deprived of the richness of the root of David. And the condition of Israel in the world today is attributed to their unbelief, which had cut them off from the help of the right arm of the Lord.

Prayer

HEAVENLY Father, deal not with me after my sins, negligences and ignorance. Cleanse my fouled soul and defiled garments. Put all my sins behind thee into the depths of the sea. Deliver me from the dominion and love of sin. Cause all grace to abound towards me, that I may have all sufficiency for all things and abound to every good work. Amen.

Lifegiver for Moribund Man

37

For he shall grow up before him as a tender plant, and as a root out of a dry ground: he hath no form nor comeliness; and when we shall see him, there is no beauty that we should desire him — *Isaiah 53:2.*

THE one aim for each of us should be to bring Christ and the dead Lazarus together. Death can no more exist when He is present than night when the sun is rising. Corruption, impurity, sin, flee before him to whom the Father gave to have life in himself. Let your faith make an inlet for the Lifegiver into your circle of society, your church, your class, your home. Nothing will suffice if this is lacking. Eloquence, learning, position, these will fail. But faith, though it be of the weakest, simplest nature, will link the Saviour, who is alive for evermore, and has the keys of death and Hades.

Let us ask Christ to work such faith in us; to develop it by every method of education and discipline; to mature it by his nurturing Spirit, until the arm of God is revealed in us and through us, and the glory of God is manifested before the gaze of men.

Prayer

ALMIGHTY God, let the leaves of the Tree of Life be for my healing and let thy peace settle upon my harassed nature. Minister nourishment to the fainting and comfort to those who have failed. Temper the gladness of success with the humility which attributes all glory and honor to thy sufficient grace. Be thou the Alpha and the Omega of every year, day, and act of my life. Let all things be begun, continued, and ended in thee. Amen.

Contrasts of the Cross

38

> But he was wounded for our transgressions, he was bruised for our iniquities: the chastisement of our peace was upon him; and with his stripes we are healed—*Isaiah 53:5.*

IT is strange that the darkest day that ever broke upon our world was destined to cure the sadness and dissipate the darkness forever. It is for this reason doubtless that Scripture lays such stress on the wondrous cross and that prophets and evangelists proceed with such deliberation to tell the story of that death, which is the death of death for all who understand its inner meaning.

With what elaborate care the meaning of the cross is wrought out in this chapter under our consideration! We are reminded that the death of our Lord was no ordinary episode but distinguished from all other deaths—the one perfect sacrifice for the sins of man. Every form of expression is used to accentuate the thought that its excessive agony was not the symptom of special sin on the part of the sufferer, but that "he was wounded for our transgressions."

Prayer

MAY I not only find forgiveness in thy cross, my blessed Lord, but may it produce in me rivers of living water. May I be satisfied not merely with talking about thy love, but in manifesting it in great crises as well as amid petty annoyances and the daily fret. Amen.

The Sinless Exception

39

And he made his grave with the wicked, and with the rich in his death; because he had done no violence, neither was any deceit in his mouth — *Isaiah 53:9.*

THE suffering Servant presents a noble exception to the lot of man; not in his sufferings, for he was a Man of Sorrows; not in his death, but in his perfect innocence and goodness. Let us consider this and the conclusion to be derived from it.

There is sorrow in this chapter, as in all the world. The marred face tells a true tale; for the turbid streams of the unknown sorrows have poured into the sufferer's heart. Despised and rejected, wounded and bruised, led to the slaughter and cut off from the land of the living amid degradation and cruelty, the Lord passed through every painful experience and studied deeply every volume in the library of pain.

This is the great exception. It may be that in a lower sense there is other suffering that is redemptive; though no sufferer is free from sin as Christ was, and none has ever been able to expiate sin as he. None can ransom his brother's soul.

Prayer

GIVE me grace, O Lord, to be watchful
against the earliest and most insidious ap-
proach—of temptation, that I may at once
hide myself under the shadow of thy wings.
Help me to walk in the footsteps of the
Christ, denying myself and becoming poor
that those around me may be made rich.
Teach me how to gain by giving and to find
by losing, according to thy word. Amen.

40

Yet it pleased the Lord to bruise him; he hath put him to grief: when thou shalt make his soul an offering for sin, he shall see his seed, he shall prolong his days, and the pleasure of the Lord shall prosper in his hand — *Isaiah 53:10*.

THIS was a voluntary act to which he was nerved by the infinite love that dared to make his soul an offering for sin. What did Jesus suffer on the cross? The physical pain that wracked his body was probably hardly perceptible to him amid the pressure of those stripes with which we are healed. He was wounded not only in his flesh but in his loving heart. He was stricken because he received into his soul the penalty of human guilt. He stood before the universe charged with the sins of the race and their consequence. He was so identified with sin, its shame, suffering, and penalty, that he deemed himself forsaken by God.

In that one act of the cross he put away sin, exhausted the penalty, wiped out the guilt, and laid the foundation of a redemption which includes the whole family of man.

Think it not strange when that fiery trial comes, but rejoice that you are called to be a partaker of the sufferings of Christ, that at the revelation of his glory you may rejoice.

Prayer

ALMIGHTY God, I beseech thee to raise me from the death of sin to the life of righteousness by that same power that brought the Lord Jesus from the dead, that I may walk in newness of life and be planted in the likeness of his resurrection. Teach me not only to bear but to love thy cross. And as I take it, may I find that it is carrying me. Amen.

The Satisfaction of Christ

41

He shall see the travail of his soul, and shall be satisfied: by his knowledge shall my righteous servant justify many; for he shall bear their iniquities — Isaiah 53:11.

SATISFIED! Very few can say that word on this side of Heaven. The philosopher cannot, though he has discovered the hidden harmonies of nature and unveiled her ancient order; for his circle of light only extends the circumference of the dark unknown. Even the Christian cannot say it, since he has not yet attained, neither is already perfect. But Christ shall be satisfied and is already drinking deep draughts of the joy set before him when he endured the cross.

There is no satisfaction for those who are self-centered. We say reverently that God himself could not have known perfect blessedness unless he had been able to pour himself forth in blessing upon others. We are therefore conscious of a fitness in meeting this allusion to the satisfaction of Christ amidst these words that speak of his sacrifice unto death.

There is no satisfaction apart from love. There cannot be travail without compensating joy.

Prayer

O SAVIOUR, who goeth after that which is lost until thou findest it, teach me to minister to the needs of others. May I pitifully regard those who know thee not and whose life is one long outrage of thy forbearing love. Give me something of thy shepherd compassion and long-suffering. Amen.

The Majestic "I"

42

Therefore will I divide him a portion with the great, and he shall divide the spoil with the strong; because he hath poured out his soul unto death: and he was numbered with the transgressors; and he bare the sin of many, and made intercession for the transgressors — Isaiah 53:12.

IT is impossible to mistake the majestic personality speaking through the pronoun "I." It is the voice of God himself. It is befitting that, as he introduced his servant in the opening verses of this portraiture, so, in these closing verses, he should pronounce his verdict on his career. One can see as the chapter unfolds how the opinion of the speaker and others passes through many phases—hostility, criticism, pity—before settling in penitence and faith. In this respect it is a true delineation of the attitude of the world generally towards Jesus of Nazareth, who realized this unique ideal.

Two things are here predicted of the sin-bearer. First, that he should be great; second, that he should attain his commanding position, not as the founder of a new school of thought, nor as the leader of a social reformation, nor as possessed of exceptional saintliness—but as a sufferer.

Prayer

ALMIGHTY God, thou hast taught me to look for the time when the creation shall be made free with the glorious liberty of the sons of God. Hasten that glorious day when thine hand shall wipe tears from all faces and the former things shall have passed away. Grant unto me, though most unworthy, to sit with thee at thy table and see thee, when thou art crowned in the joy of thine espousals. Amen.

Consequences of Sin

43

Sing, O barren, thou that didst not bear; break forth into singing, and cry aloud, thou that didst not travail with child: for more are the children of the desolate than the children of the married wife, saith the Lord — *Isaiah 54:1.*

WE must differentiate between the punitive and penal effects of sin. Take the case of a man who, in his devotion to politics or society, has sinned against the laws of the home. Night after night he has been away from his young children, until they regard him as a stranger. There is none of that wholesome companionship, that abandonment of trust, which are such sacred ties. The mother cannot supply the firmness and strength which the young life needs. Almost insensibly the family grows away from him; and after a few years, when disappointment drives him back, he finds to his regret that the love of the children has gone beyond recall. The boys are now men and seek their pleasure outside the home. The girls think it irksome to while away his weary hours by their society. Now he sees his mistake and tries to remedy it; but it is too late. He is forgiven by his God and his wife who never ceased to cling to him; but he cannot get back that forfeited love. This is his ruined Jerusalem.

Prayer

O BLESSED Father, let not sin have dominion over me. If temptation assails, may it find no foothold in my heart. If I have to pass through scenes where the infection of sin is strong, may I not yield to it. Let the fire of thy love consume in me all sinful desires of the flesh and of the mind, that I may henceforth continually abide in Jesus Christ and seek the things where He sits at thy right hand. Amen.

Love Inalienable

44

For thy Maker is thine husband; The Lord of Hosts is his name; and thy Redeemer the Holy One of Israel; The God of the whole earth shall he be called — Isaiah 54:5.

WE may believe in his inalienable love. He is our husband still and cannot put us away from him; the kindness with which he has had mercy on us is everlasting. He has even sworn that the waters of death and destruction shall not forever separate us from him. He has entered into a covenant of peace with us which shall outlast the mountains and the hills. We may grow apathetic and careless, bringing to ourselves gain and woe and hindering the development of his purpose. But he cannot cease to love. His tender pity will still embrace us, grieving to see our self-inflicted sorrows. If I ascend into heaven, thy love is there; but if I make my bed in hell, it is there also. If I take the wings of the morning, and dwell in the uttermost part of the sea, placing it as a great gulf of separation between thee and me, there shall thy hand lead me and thy right hand uphold me.

Prayer

GRACIOUS Father, I thank thee for the Son of thy love, for all that he has done for us and will do; for all that he had been to us and will be. Teach me to trust thy love. May I dare to believe it when the dark clouds brood, as well as when the sun shines. May I never doubt that thou art doing thy best for me and that what I know not now, I shall know hereafter. Amen.

Taught of God

45

And all thy children shall be taught of the Lord; and great shall be the peace of thy children — *Isaiah 54:13.*

IT is a deep and helpful thought that God has opened a school in this dark world and has himself undertaken to act as schoolmaster. He delegates to no inferior hand the sublime work of educating the human soul. But fear not, it is the Father who teaches. He knows our frame and remembers that we are dust.

How often, when we were at school in the long spring days, our eyes have strayed from book or slate. We have heard, but not learned and the lesson has been turned back. Oh, the irksomeness of those turned lessons, when all nature awaited us outside. So do we evade these divine lessons, given on the pages of Scripture, of conscience, and inculcated by a divine tenderness. Did we truly learn of the Father we should inevitably get to the feet of Jesus.

When men say they believe in God but not in Jesus Christ they depart from the truth.

Prayer

O LORD, who didst illuminate the heart of Thomas with the clear radiance of thy risen glory, thou knowest how to deal with the doubts and perplexities of my heart. I have not seen; give me the blessedness of those who have believed. I desire to take on me thy yoke and to learn thy way. Teach me to rejoice always; to pray without ceasing; and in everything to give thanks. Amen.

God Rules and Overrules

46

No weapon that is formed against thee shall prosper; and every tongue that shall rise against thee in judgment thou shalt condemn. This is the heritage of the servants of the Lord, and their righteousness is of me, saith the Lord — *Isaiah 54:17.*

THE waster fulfills a function: the knife that cuts away the dead wood, the fire that eats out the alloy, the fan that rids the wheat of the chaff, the frost crumbling up the soil, the vast herds of animals that devour and destroy. This is the strong Hebrew way of saying that God permits and overrules and brings out good by means of the evil that had seemed destructive of all good.

Think it not strange concerning the fiery trials which you face. Do not seek to vindicate or avenge yourself. Be still and know that your God reigns. He will interpose at the exact hour of need. He will vindicate. He will turn the edge of the weapons of your foes against themselves and silence the accusing, calumniating voice. This is your heritage. If you are his servant, your honor is in the divine keeping.

Prayer

HEAVENLY Father, I pray thee to give
us faith in thy guardian care. May we realize that we are surrounded by hosts of
watching angels. Bless and defend and save
all whom we love, that they and we may
be conscious partakers of thy heavenly
benediction. There are so many mysteries
in the world and in human life that my
eyes are tired of straining in the dark. I
can only follow on to know thee. Yet I believe that thy going forth is prepared as
the morning. In the meanwhile refresh my
heart as the rain. Amen.

Beyond Price

47

Ho, every one that thirsteth, come ye to the waters, and he that hath no money; come ye, buy, and eat; yea, come, buy wine and milk without money and without price — Isaiah 55:1.

IT was highly necessary that God should call the attention of the Jewish people to these unpurchasable possessions. Their life in Babylon had become rather luxurious. They had so suddenly acquired wealth, bartering their spiritual prerogative for mercenary considerations, that there was the danger of their losing sight of the great facts of the spiritual world. It was needful therefore for them to be reminded that the immortal thirst of the soul cannot be quenched by waters whose source is in the depth of the earth, though the wells be as deep as Sychar's; and that its hunger cannot be satisfied with the provision beneath which the tables of a Dives groan.

True satisfaction—that which is really bread—can only be obtained where the coins of this world do not pass current; in fellowship with him whose voice is ever speaking in the marts of commerce, saying: "Ho, every one that thirsteth, come ye to the waters."

Prayer

O TRUE vine of God, I desire to abide in thee, that the sap of thy life, passing through my life, may bear abundant fruit for thy glory. Thou art all I want. Feed me with thy flesh and blood, according to thy promise, for they are meat and drink indeed, so that thou mayest live in me and I in thee in close and ever closer union. Amen.

The Divine Call

48

Behold, thou shalt call a nation that thou knowest not, and nations that knew not thee shall run unto thee, because of the Lord thy God, and for the Holy One of Israel; for he hath glorified thee — Isaiah 55:5.

THOU shall call a nation that thou knowest not—" To whom can this refer except to the Gentiles, who were once far off? "Nations that knew not thee shall run unto thee—" Of whom can this be true but of that vast ingathering suggested to our Lord by the Greeks who came to him before he died, and concerning whom he said, "I, if I be lifted up, will draw all men unto me."

These words are a direct address from the people of God to their directly given leader. Thankfully they remind him that the Holy One of Israel has glorified him. And when did our Lord receive honor and glory except when he received a name which is above every name?

God has given—will you accept his gift? He gave his only Son and with him will freely give us all things. Draw near and let him be your comfort, assurance, and salvation, world without end.

Prayer

O GLORIOUS Leader of faithful souls, who hast conducted an exodus from the grave and the dark domain of selfishness and sin, we pray that nations who have not known thee may run to thee; that there may be a great gathering of the peoples around thy banner; and that many who are wasting their energy for waters that cannot quench their thirst and for bread that cannot satisfy their hunger, may follow thee to the river of the water of life. Amen.

The Road Back

49

Let the wicked forsake his way, and the un-righteous man his thoughts: and let him return unto the Lord, and he will have mercy upon him; and to our God, for he will abundantly pardon — *Isaiah 55:7.*

IT is impossible for the natural man to please God. God's thoughts are holiness, his ways purity; but those of the unregenerate are unholy and impure. God's thoughts are love, his ways tenderness; but those of the unregenerate are self-centered and injurious. God's thoughts are truth, his ways faithful; while those of the unregenerate are insincere. How impossible it is then for those in the flesh to please God!

It is imperative therefore that the ways and thoughts of the wicked be forsaken. The eyes that had been fixed on vanity must be lifted in the track of the ascending Lord; the feet that had almost gone over the precipice to perdition must run in the way of God's will, that God may work in it that which is pleasing in his sight for the glory of his Holy Name.

Prayer

LORD, I thank thee for the pillar of cloud by day and of fire by night. May I never go in front or loiter behind. When it moves in the path of duty or suffering, help me to follow; when it stays, teach me to take and use gladly the rest which thou givest. When the storms are high, may I feel thee near; as thou camest through the mist and across the storm-swept waves, saying—"It is I; be not afraid." Amen.

Human and Divine Forgiveness

50

For as the heavens are higher than the earth, so are my ways higher than your ways, and my thoughts than your thoughts — *Isaiah 55:9*.

THERE is no parallel between our forgiveness and God's. We must not measure his by ours. We say we would forgive if there were more adequate contrition, more complete confession. Or we would forgive if the sin were not so willful and unprovoked; or we will forgive but not forget. Our forgiveness is not ready and we are often cautious and chilly towards those who have offended us, but to whom we have become reconciled.

Leave your miserable standards behind, whether of your own forgiveness or of those of others. They positively will not help you out here; your fathoming lines are utterly useless, your estimates futile. Measure the height of yonder heavens above the earth and then begin to compute the abundance of God's pardon to those who return to him with confession on their lips and true penitence in their hearts.

Prayer

HOLY Father, I thank thee for thy forgiving, pitying love. I gratefully realize that our sin cannot alter thy love, though it may dim our enjoyment of it. But I intreat thee to set me free from the love and power of sin, that it may not intercept the light of thy countenance. Quicken me by thy Holy Spirit, I pray thee, that I may run in the way that thou hast marked out for me, with enlarged desire. May I ever be looking unto Jesus. Amen.

Restoration at Last

51

For ye shall go out with joy, and be led forth with peace: the mountains and the hills shall break forth before you into singing, and all the trees of the field shall clap their hands — *Isaiah 55:12*.

THE wealth of God's abundant pardon is here set forth in metaphors which the least imaginative can understand. Not only were the exiles forgiven, their warfare accomplished, but they would be restored to the land of their fathers. Not only were they to be restored; but their return was to be one long triumphal march. Nature herself would celebrate it with joyful demonstration; mountains and hills would break forth into singing.

But even this was not all. One of the necessary results of the depopulation of Israel was the deterioration of the soil. Vast tracts had passed out of cultivation, the terraces had become heaps of stones. But this too was to be reversed. Literally and metaphorically there was to be a complete reversal of the results of the former sins and backslidings. This would be an everlasting sign that would not be cut off.

Prayer

O LORD Jesus, hasten the time of the general homecoming, when we shall no longer be strangers and pilgrims, but enter in by the gates of the city and meet again with our beloved. Send, we beseech of thee, thy Holy Spirit upon the world in mighty power to convict men of sin and righteousness and judgment. May he work again as at Pentecost. Amen.

52

Instead of the thorn shall come up the fir tree, and instead of the brier shall come up the myrtle tree: and it shall be to the Lord for a name — Isaiah 55:13.

THE grace of God actually tranforms awkward and evil dispositions, both in ourselves and others. Softness becomes meekness; cowardice, gentleness; impulsiveness, enthusiasm; meanness, thrift; niggardliness, generosity; cruelty, consideration for others. Similarly God does not destroy any of our natural characteristics when he brings us to himself. He only eliminates the evil and develops the good.

The evil tenant goes forth, making room for the new and Holy Spirit. Where sin has reigned to death, now grace reigns to eternal life. The thorns of passion and temper are replaced by fir trees and the briers of myrtles. He takes the heart of stone out of our flesh and gives us a heart of flesh.

Prayer

ALMIGHTY God, heaven and earth are
full of thy glory. Every day is a day that
thou hast made. May I hunger no more,
neither thirst any more, because I am
abundantly satisfied with the fatness of thy
house. Thine is the greatness and the power,
and the glory and the victory, for all that
is in Heaven and earth is thine. Thine is
the kingdom, O God. Thou art exalted above
all. Glory be to thee. Amen.